CELEBRATING TEXAS

Patriotic Symbols and Landmarks

Trisha James

PowerKiDS press™

NEW YORK

Published in 2010 by The Rosen Publishing Group, Inc.
29 East 21st Street, New York, NY 10010

Copyright © 2010 by The Rosen Publishing Group, Inc.

Book Design: Daniel Hosek

Photo Credits: Cover (cattle), pp. 21, 28 (Johnson) Time & Life Pictures/Getty Images; cover (meteor), p. 23 (meteor impact) Max Dannenbaum/Stone/Getty Images; cover (River Walk), pp. 26–27 Panoramic Images/Getty Images; cover (flag), interior borders and backgrounds, pp. 4 (flag), 9 (bluebonnet), 11 (Alamo), 13 Shutterstock.com; cover (background map) pp. 5, 7 (map) © Geoatlas; pp. 8 (Enchanted Rock), 14 (floor with seal), 15 (seal), 17 (seal), 18 (flags), 22 (mountain), 23 (inset), 24–25 (Longhorn Cavern) Wikimedia Commons; pp. 9 (Enchanted Rock), 20 (longhorn), 25 (inset) iStockphoto.com; p. 10 (Alamo) Hulton Archive/Getty Images; p. 12 (Santa Anna) courtesy Library of Congress, Prints and Photographs Division; p. 19 (roller coaster) Darren McCollester/Getty Images; p. 29 (space center) Getty Images.

Library of Congress Cataloging-in-Publication Data

James, Trisha.
Celebrating Texas : patriotic symbols and landmarks / Trisha James.
    p. cm. — (Spotlight on Texas)
Includes index.
ISBN 978-1-61532-484-2 (pbk.)
ISBN 978-1-61532-485-9 (6-pack)
ISBN 978-1-61532-486-6 (library binding)
1. Texas—Juvenile literature. 2. Signs and symbols—Texas—Juvenile literature. I. Title.
F386.3.J363 2010
976.4—dc22

2009037934

Manufactured in the United States of America

CPSIA Compliance Information: Batch # WW1ORC: For further information contact Rosen Publishing, New York, New York at 1-800-237-9932.

CONTENTS

TEXAS: SO MUCH TO CELEBRATE

Texas has one of the most exciting histories of any state in the nation. Native Americans, Spanish, French, Mexicans, English, and many others have called Texas home. Because of its interesting past, Texas has many buildings, objects, and places that people like to visit. These are called landmarks. Landmarks may be natural or made by people.

Texans are patriotic, which means they are proud and loyal to their state. They celebrate, or honor, Texas and its many landmarks and **symbols**. Learning more about these landmarks and symbols helps us learn more about Texas's past and present. We also learn why we should celebrate Texas, too!

1690—Alonso De León is first European to follow El Camino Real de los Tejas.

April 21, 1836—Battle of San Jacinto fought.

1839—Republic of Texas adopts "lone star" flag.

March 6, 1836—Battle of the Alamo fought.

December 10, 1836—Republic of Texas adopts seal.

1841—John Coffee Hays fights Comanches on Enchanted Rock.

Texas is the second-largest state in the United States. It's also the second most populated.

Odessa Crater

Six Flags Over Texas Park

Fort Worth

Odessa

Enchanted Rock

Fort Stockton

Burnet

Longhorn Cavern

Fredericksburg

Houston

San Antonio

Alamo

Johnson Space Center

San Jacinto Monument

Paseo del Rio

Kingsville

King Ranch

1852—Richard King camps at Santa Gertrudis Creek.

1901—Bluebonnet becomes Texas state flower.

1939—San Jacinto Monument completed.

1992—Current Texas state seal is adopted.

1892—Julius Henderson sees Odessa Meteor Crater.

1932—Longhorn Cavern becomes a state park.

1969—Apollo 11 lands on moon.

A VERY LONG LANDMARK

One of the oldest landmarks in Texas is more than 2,500 miles (4,000 km) long! El Camino Real de los Tejas is a trail across Texas. Its name is Spanish for "Royal Road of the Friends." The word "tejas" probably comes from a Native American word meaning "friends." The road is also often called Old San Antonio Road. The road is actually several connected roads and trails. They reach from west of the Rio Grande to east of the Sabine River.

The history of El Camino Real goes back to before Europeans arrived. Native Americans used paths to travel between settlements and to find food. When the Spanish arrived, they used these paths, too. In 1690, Alonso De León followed the Native American paths to set up the first Spanish **mission** in east Texas. More missions followed, bringing more settlers. El Camino Real became a path between missions. It was used to move supplies, for trade, and for the military.

The different trails of El Camino Real de los Tejas changed with weather, nature, and how well settlers and Native Americans were getting along.

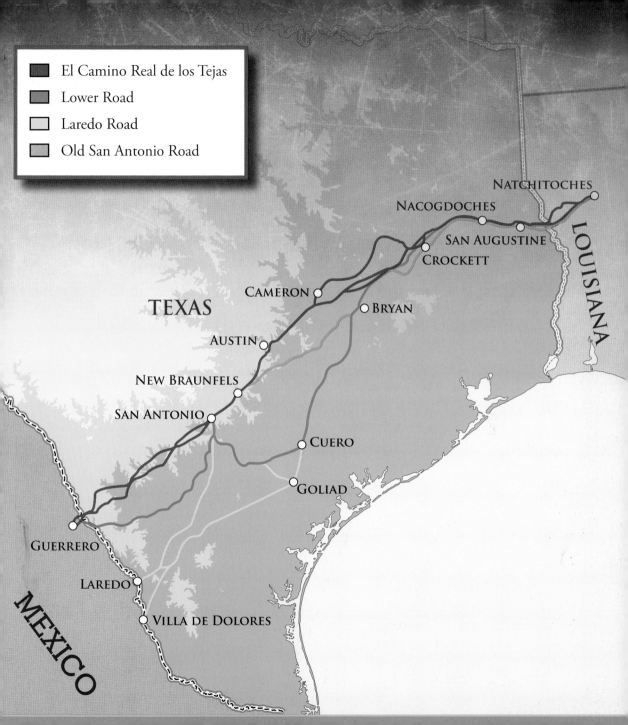

ENCHANTED ROCK

Another Texas landmark's fame began with Native American stories. Europeans heard these tales of a huge, pinkish rock called Enchanted Rock. Enchanted Rock is about 20 miles (32 km) north of Fredericksburg, Texas. It's about 425 feet (130 m) high and covers about 640 acres!

Many stories tell of Enchanted Rock's magic and of Native American ghosts haunting the rock. A marker on the rock tells about an event that occurred in 1841. Texas soldier John Coffee Hays fought off many Comanche Indians by himself. Some say the Comanches finally ran away, thinking the rock's magic was helping him.

This is a view from the top of Enchanted Rock.

These tales may come from the way the rock shines and makes noises at night. Scientists say the shine is from moonlight shining on water drops trapped between bits of rock. They think the noises happen as the hot rock cools at night.

Early European settlers saw the shine of Enchanted Rock and believed it was silver or iron. However, it's made of a rock called pink granite.

The Texas State Flower

The bluebonnet is a natural symbol of Texas. These purplish blue flowers grow all over Texas in the spring. The bluebonnet became the state flower in 1901.

LANDMARKS OF THE REVOLUTION

Many of the most famous Texas landmarks and symbols came from the **Texas Revolution**. Perhaps the best known is the Alamo. The Alamo is another name for the San Antonio de Valero Mission in San Antonio. Built in the early 1700s, the mission was a center of Catholic faith and community. In the 1800s, it was used as a military fort.

Some famous soldiers at the Battle of the Alamo included William Barret Travis, James Bowie, and David (or Davy) Crockett. Only about 200 Texans stood against about 4,000 Mexican troops. "Remember the

During the Texas Revolution, a major battle was fought at the Alamo. In February 1836, Mexican ruler and general Antonio López de Santa Anna marched into San Antonio. He wanted to stop Texas from gaining independence. A group of Texans gathered within the Alamo and refused to give up. On March 6, the Mexican army fought their way into the Alamo. No Texas fighters inside the Alamo were left alive.

Some landmarks are so important they are both a landmark and a symbol. The Alamo is one of these. To many, it's a symbol of Texas.

The last battle of the Texas Revolution was the Battle of San Jacinto. After the Alamo fell, Santa Anna forced the Texans into eastern Texas. On April 21, 1836, Texas general Sam Houston surprised Santa Anna near the San Jacinto River. The Texans defeated the Mexican forces in under half an hour! Santa Anna agreed to end the war and let Texas be an independent country.

To honor that **victory**, a monument was built at the battle site between 1936 and 1939. It's 570 feet (174 m) tall, has eight sides, and is made of rock. A **museum** was built at the base of the San Jacinto Monument. The story of Texas is written on its walls.

Antonio López de Santa Anna

The San Jacinto Monument is the tallest war monument in the world!

13

THE SYMBOLS OF THE TEXAS SEAL

You may have heard Texas called the "Lone Star State." A single star with five points has been a symbol of Texas since Texas won its revolution. The first government of the **Republic** of Texas chose the star to stand for their new country. It was a reminder that Texas stood alone but with pride.

In 1836, the new nation created its first seal. A seal is a symbol placed on government papers and other official property. Although the seal has been changed many times over the years, the "lone star" has always been on it. Today's Texas state seal has an oak branch that stands for strength to the left of the star. To the right is an olive branch that stands for peace.

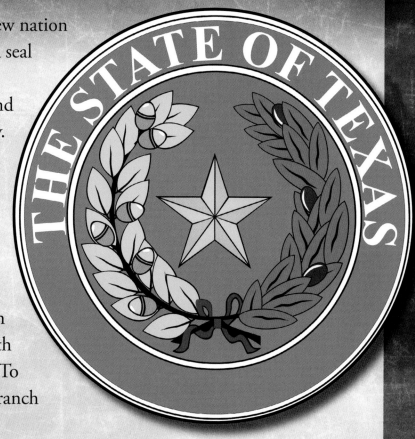

The first seal of Texas had the words "Republic of Texas." When Texas became part of the United States in 1845, the words were changed to "The State of Texas."

In 1961, the Texas state government approved symbols for the back of the seal. The lone star appears again at the top. In the middle of the seal are three important symbols of the Texas Revolution. The Alamo appears below the lone star, with the words "Remember the Alamo" above it. On the bottom left is a cannon. At the Battle of Gonzales, Texans refused to give their cannon to the Mexican army. To the right of the cannon is a bridge that has come to be called Vince's Bridge. It was the only way of escape for Santa Anna's army at the Battle of San Jacinto. The Texans burned it, which trapped Santa Anna's soldiers and helped the Texans win the battle. Around these pictures are six flags that stand for the countries that ruled some or all of Texas at one time.

The official state seal is in Austin, the state capital. It is kept by the secretary of state. The back of the seal is pictured here. The words "Texas One and Indivisible" mean that Texas can't be divided into parts.

REMEMBER THE ALAMO

TEXAS ONE AND INDIVISIBLE

THE SIX FLAGS OF TEXAS

Together, the "six flags over Texas" form a symbol of Texas's interesting past. The flags of France, Spain, Mexico, the Republic of Texas, the **Confederate States of America**, and the United States are signs of the rich history of Texas.

In the 1500s and 1600s, France and Spain claimed land in Mexico, which included Texas. Then, in 1821, Mexico won independence from Spain. The Texas Revolution ended in 1836 with Texas becoming independent. Finally, in 1845, Texas became part of the United States. From 1861 to 1865, Texas sided with the Confederate States of America during the American Civil War. It later rejoined the United States.

Where the Fun Began

A famous amusement park in Texas uses the name "Six Flags Over Texas." This park was originally made up of six areas named for the six flags of Texas. You can learn more about the history of Texas in each area. Other areas have since been added to the park. Later, other amusement parks around the United States began using the name "Six Flags," too.

KING ★ RANCH

In the 1800s, many people settled in Texas to raise livestock. Texas became famous for its ranches. In 1852, riverboat captain Richard King was riding his horse across southern Texas. He camped near Santa Gertrudis Creek. King and his friend Gideon Lewis began buying land along the creek. After Lewis died in 1855, King continued buying land. The King Ranch raised horses, sheep, and goats, and was especially known for its cattle. King hired cowboys to care for the livestock.

After King's death in 1885, later owners began more businesses at King Ranch. In the mid-1900s, the ranch produced winning racehorses. After oil and gas were found on the ranch, these became businesses, too. The King Ranch is one of the leading businesses in Texas today.

Texas longhorn

Today's King Ranch is 825,000 acres! That's larger than the state of Rhode Island! The Texas longhorn cow, shown above, was named an official symbol of Texas by the state government in 1995.

METEORITES IN TEXAS!

Some other Texas landmarks actually came from space! Near Odessa in 1892, rancher Julius Henderson was looking for a lost calf. He came upon a wide area that was lower than the surrounding ground. Although he didn't know it, he had found a meteor **crater**. A meteor is a space rock that burns as it approaches Earth. When it hits the ground, it's called a meteorite. Scientists think a large meteorite landed near Odessa more than 50,000 years ago. The crash caused the rock to explode and made the giant crater.

Scientists studying hills near Fort Stockton in western Texas believe another meteorite landed there perhaps 100 million years ago! The crash was so powerful it pushed up rock to form a mountain about 5 miles (8 km) across and 4,593 feet (1,400 m) high.

mountain formed by the meteorite that landed near Fort Stockton

CROSS SECTION OF CRATER...

1. LATEST SILT & SAND
2. OLDER SILT, SAND, CALICHE, & PEBBLES
3. FRAGMENTAL ROCK
4. ROCK FLOUR
5. SHAFT·165' DEEP

The Odessa Meteor Crater is actually several craters. The largest crater covers 10 acres. As you can see in this cross section sign, much of the crater has been hidden from view over the years. The hole was once 100 feet (30 m) deep!

LONGHORN CAVERN

Another natural Texas landmark has been used in many surprising ways over the years. Longhorn **Cavern** is located about 9 miles (14 km) southwest of Burnet. A group of hills formed there millions of years ago. Water dripping through the rock slowly made bigger and bigger holes within the hills over time. The holes became so big that they formed huge rooms.

We know from bones found there that ancient animals used Longhorn Cavern. Comanche Indians used the rock found in the cavern to make tools. In the 1860s, Confederate soldiers used the cavern as a place to make gunpowder, which they needed to fire their weapons. Some say outlaws used it as a place to hide. In the 1920s and 1930s, the cavern was even used as a dance hall!

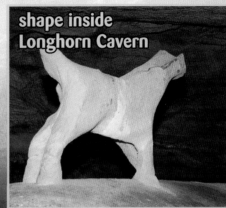

shape inside Longhorn Cavern

Only 11 miles (18 km) of Longhorn Cavern have been explored. In 1932, Longhorn Cavern became a state park.

SAN ANTONIO RIVER WALK

In the 1900s, Texans began moving into cities such as San Antonio to live and work. In September 1921, the San Antonio River flooded, killing about fifty people. The city government hired **engineers** to stop this from happening again. The engineers built a dam, which was finished in 1927.

Each year, about 80,000 new plants line the River Walk.

The engineers also wanted to build a street over parts of the river. Some people living in the city disagreed. They showed the city officials that the river could be deepened and cleaned. Walkways and gardens could be planted along it. The Paseo del Rio, or "River Walk," was completed in March 1941.

Today, people from all over the world come to San Antonio to visit this beautiful river. They shop and eat along the 2.5-mile (4-km) path. As many as 1 million people ride boats on the river each year!

JOHNSON SPACE CENTER

Another Texas landmark is still making news. The Johnson Space Center is 30 miles (48 km) south of Houston. It's made up of 142 buildings. More than 19,000 people work there!

In 1961, President John F. Kennedy set a goal to land a manned American spacecraft on the moon. To do this, **NASA** needed a new manned spacecraft center. Houston, Texas, was the chosen place.

Lyndon B. Johnson, Texan and President

In the 1950s, Lyndon B. Johnson represented Texas in the U.S. Senate. As a senator, he began working toward space exploration. In 1960, Johnson became John F. Kennedy's vice president. When Kennedy was killed in 1963, Johnson became the first U.S. president from Texas. After Johnson died in 1973, the Houston space center was renamed to honor him.

Several spacecraft called *Apollo* were **launched** from Houston. They prepared for the final goal—a moon landing. On July 20, 1969, *Apollo 11* completed the goal. Neil A. Armstrong was the first man to walk on the moon.

Now you've read about some of the most interesting Texas landmarks and symbols. You can see why Texans have so many reasons to celebrate their amazing state!

TEXAS LANDMARKS

LANDMARK	NATURAL	MAN-MADE
El Camino Real de los Tejas		X
Alamo		X
Enchanted Rock	X	
King Ranch		X
Longhorn Cavern	X	
Odessa Meteor Crater	X	
San Jacinto Monument		X
Paseo del Rio	X	X
Johnson Space Center		X

Reader Response Projects

- Read more about the *Apollo* space missions. Make a timeline of one of the missions on poster board. On your timeline, write dates and facts telling what the mission was meant to accomplish, what happened on the mission, and any other interesting facts.

- There are many more Texas landmarks. Use the library and Internet to find more landmarks you'd like to visit. Draw a blank map of Texas. Label the landmarks on the map. Be ready to tell others what happened at these landmarks.

- At the library or on the Internet, find a Native American story about Enchanted Rock. Write the story in your own words to create a book. Draw or find pictures that help tell your story. Share your story with your class.

- Look at the Texas state seal. Think of what you would draw or write on a seal that is meant to be a symbol of you. Draw your seal. Then ask a friend to draw a symbol of you. Compare the symbols.

GLOSSARY

cavern (KA-vuhrn) A large cave found under the ground.

Confederate States of America (kuhn-FEH-duh-ruht STAYTS UV uh-MEHR-uh-kuh) A group of Southern states that announced themselves separate from the United States in 1860 and 1861.

crater (KRAY-tuhr) A large bowl-shaped hole in the ground.

engineer (ehn-juh-NIHR) A person who plans and builds engines, machines, roads, and bridges.

launch (LAWNCH) To forcefully push out or put into the air or water.

mission (MIH-shun) A place where church leaders teach their beliefs and help the community.

museum (myoo-ZEE-uhm) A place where objects of art or history are safely kept for people to see and study.

NASA (NAA-suh) National Aeronautics and Space Administration, the United States' government office in charge of studying space.

republic (rih-PUH-blihk) A form of government in which the authority belongs to the people and they pick the government leaders.

symbol (SIHM-buhl) Something that stands for something else.

Texas Revolution (TEHK-suhs reh-vuh-LOO-shun) The war fought by settlers in Texas to win their freedom from Mexico.

victory (VIHK-tuh-ree) A win against an enemy.

INDEX

Due to the changing nature of Internet links, the Rosen Publishing Group, Inc., has developed an online list of Web sites related to the subject of this book. This site is updated regularly. Please use this link to access the list: **http://www.rcbmlinks.com/sot/symland/**